The CSS Grid Guidebook

THE CSS GRID GUIDEBOOK

All You Need to Understand the Grid Layout Module in CSS

Oluwatobi Sofela

CODESWEETLY

THE CSS GRID GUIDEBOOK

Front Cover Floral Pattern Illustrator: Satheesh Sankaran

First edition. February 24, 2023.

www.codesweetly.com

C⟨8⟩DESWEETLY

Contents

Contents

Introduction

Welcome to CSS Grid!

CSS Grid gives you the tools to create basic and advanced website layouts in flexible and responsive ways.

This book will use images and live examples to discuss everything you need to know to use CSS Grid like a pro.

How This Book Can Help You Understand CSS Grid

The best way to learn is through progressive practice. In other words, the easiest way to understand CSS Grid is to proactively try out Grid's concepts—rather than merely reading or watching videos about them.

As such, this book is intentionally examples-oriented to get you to practice as much as possible while learning the fundamental concepts of CSS Grid.

Therefore, you will do yourself much favor by opening your text editor (such as VS Code) and trying out the concepts explained herein. By so doing, you will avoid being part of those stuck in "Tutorial Hell."

Book's Style

This book (The CSS Grid Guidebook) goes straight to the point to explain each concept. It uses a short, simple, and direct explanation style. So, consider it as your quick and comprehensive reference guide to CSS Grid.

Prerequisite

Familiarity with HTML and CSS will help you learn CSS Grid better. So, to be better prepared for this book's content, it's best to be familiar with the elementary aspect of those two languages.

Using Live Examples

Whenever you come across a "Live Example[3]" text, it means there is an associated Stackblitz link where you will find a working demo.

You can visit the "Endnote" section at the end of this book to get the live demo's URL.

Note that the superscript number placed at the end of the "Live Example[3]" text references the text's associated endnote.

Questions and Comments

For questions and comments about this book, email contact@codesweetly.com or send me a direct message on Twitter (@oluwatobiss).

Let's Get It Started!

In the following chapter, you will learn what CSS Grid is and why people use it.

CSS Grid

The CSS Grid Layout Module makes browsers display the selected HTML elements as grid <u>box models</u>[1].

Grid allows easy resizing and repositioning of a grid container and its items two-dimensionally.

Note:

- "Two-dimensionally" means grid modules allow simultaneous laying out of box models in rows and columns.

- Use <u>flexbox</u>[2] if you only need to resize and reposition elements one-dimensionally.

Grid Container

A grid container (the large area below) is an <u>HTML element</u>[3] whose <u>display</u>[4] property's value is grid or inline-grid.

Grid Items

Grid items (the smaller boxes within the large container) are the direct children of a grid container.

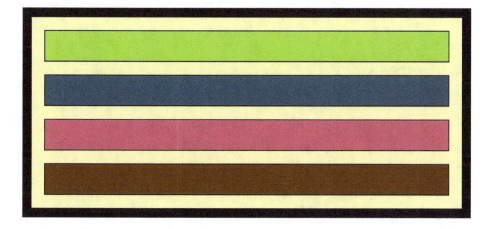

display: grid

grid tells browsers to display the selected HTML element as a block-level[5] grid box model.

Converting a node to a grid box model makes the element's direct children become grid items.

Try it yourself

CSS

```css
section {
  display: grid;
  background-color: orange;
  margin: 10px;
  padding: 7px;
}

div {
  background-color: purple;
  color: white;
  margin: 5px;
  padding: 10px;
  border-radius: 5px;
}
```

HTML

```html
<section>
  <div>1</div>
  <div>2</div>
  <div>3</div>
  <div>4</div>
</section>
<section>
  <div>5</div>
  <div>6</div>
  <div>7</div>
  <div>8</div>
</section>
```

Live Example[7]

display: inline-grid

inline-grid tells browsers to display the selected HTML element as an inline-level[6] grid box model.

The display: inline-grid directive only affects a box model and its direct children. It does not affect grandchildren nodes.

Try it yourself

CSS

```
section {
  display: inline-grid;
  background-color: orange;
  margin: 10px;
  padding: 7px;
}

div {
  background-color: purple;
  color: white;
  margin: 5px;
  padding: 10px;
  border-radius: 5px;
}
```

HTML

```
<section>
  <div>1</div>
  <div>2</div>
  <div>3</div>
  <div>4</div>
</section>
<section>
  <div>5</div>
  <div>6</div>
  <div>7</div>
  <div>8</div>
</section>
```

Live Example[8]

"Never be discouraged when you make progress, no matter how slow or small. Only be wary of standing still."

– John Mason

Grid Containers Properties

A grid container's properties specify how browsers should layout items within the grid box model.

We define a grid container's property on the grid container, not its items.

Types of grid container properties

1. grid-template-columns

2. grid-template-rows

3. grid-auto-columns

4. grid-auto-rows

5. justify-content

6. justify-items

7. align-content

8. align-items

grid-template-columns

grid-template-columns specifies the number and widths of columns browsers should display in the selected grid container.

Try it yourself

CSS

```css
section {
  display: grid;
  grid-template-columns: 15% 60% 25%;
  background-color: orange;
  margin: 10px;
  padding: 7px;
}

div {
  background-color: purple;
  color: white;
  margin: 5px;
  padding: 10px;
  border-radius: 5px;
}
```

HTML

```html
<section>
  <div>1</div>
  <div>2</div>
  <div>3</div>
  <div>4</div>
  <div>5</div>
  <div>6</div>
  <div>7</div>
  <div>8</div>
  <div>9</div>
  <div>10</div>
  <div>11</div>
  <div>12</div>
</section>
```

Live Example[9]

grid-template-rows

`grid-template-rows` specifies the number and heights of rows browsers should display in the selected grid container.

Try it yourself

CSS

```css
section {
  display: grid;
  grid-template-rows: 90px 300px 1fr;
  grid-template-columns: auto auto auto auto;
  background-color: orange;
  margin: 10px;
  padding: 7px;
}

div {
  background-color: purple;
  color: white;
  margin: 5px;
  padding: 10px;
  border-radius: 5px;
}
```

HTML

```html
<section>
  <div>1</div>
  <div>2</div>
  <div>3</div>
  <div>4</div>
  <div>5</div>
  <div>6</div>
  <div>7</div>
  <div>8</div>
  <div>9</div>
  <div>10</div>
  <div>11</div>
  <div>12</div>
</section>
```

Live Example[10]

YOUR FREE GIFT

As a thank you for buying my book, I would like to give you my Git Cheat Sheet **100% FREE!**

<u>DOWNLOAD IT HERE</u>:

https://www.subscribepage.com/git-cheatsheet

justify-content Property

justify-content specifies how browsers should position a grid container's columns along its row axis.

Note:

- A row axis is sometimes called an inline axis.

- The justify-content property works only if the total column widths are less than the grid container's width. In other words, you need free space along the container's row axis to justify its columns left or right.

justify-content property's values

1. start

2. center

3. end

4. stretch

5. space-between

6. space-around

7. space-evenly

justify-content: start

start positions the grid container's columns with its row-start edge.

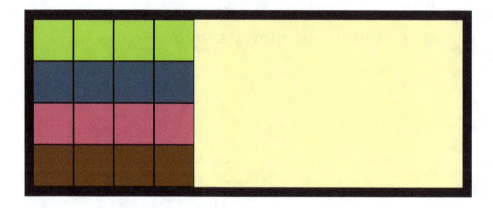

Try it yourself

CSS

```css
section {
  display: grid;
  justify-content: start;
  grid-template-columns: repeat(4, 40px);
  background-color: orange;
  margin: 10px;
}

div {
  border: 1px solid black;
  background-color: purple;
  color: white;
  padding: 10px;
  border-radius: 5px;
  text-align: center;
}
```

HTML

```html
<section>
  <div>1</div>
  <div>2</div>
  <div>3</div>
  <div>4</div>
  <div>5</div>
  <div>6</div>
  <div>7</div>
  <div>8</div>
</section>
```

Live Example[11]

justify-content: center

center positions the grid container's columns to the center of the grid's row axis.

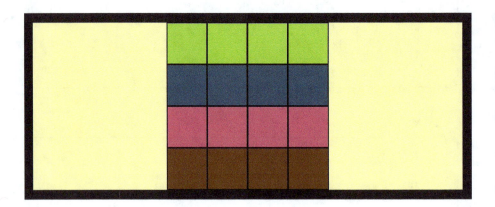

Try it yourself

CSS

```css
section {
  display: grid;
  justify-content: center;
  grid-template-columns: repeat(4, 40px);
  background-color: orange;
  margin: 10px;
}

div {
  border: 1px solid black;
  background-color: purple;
  color: white;
  padding: 10px;
  border-radius: 5px;
  text-align: center;
}
```

HTML

```html
<section>
  <div>1</div>
  <div>2</div>
  <div>3</div>
  <div>4</div>
  <div>5</div>
  <div>6</div>
  <div>7</div>
  <div>8</div>
</section>
```

Live Example[12]

justify-content: end

end positions a grid container's columns with its row-end edge.

Try it yourself

CSS

```css
section {
  display: grid;
  justify-content: end;
  grid-template-columns: repeat(4, 40px);
  background-color: orange;
  margin: 10px;
}

div {
  border: 1px solid black;
  background-color: purple;
  color: white;
  padding: 10px;
  border-radius: 5px;
  text-align: center;
}
```

HTML

```html
<section>
  <div>1</div>
  <div>2</div>
  <div>3</div>
  <div>4</div>
  <div>5</div>
  <div>6</div>
  <div>7</div>
  <div>8</div>
</section>
```

Live Example[13]

justify-content: space-between

`space-between` does the following:

- It positions a grid container's first column with its row-start edge.

- It positions the container's last column with the row-end edge.

- It creates even spacing between each pair of columns between the first and last columns.

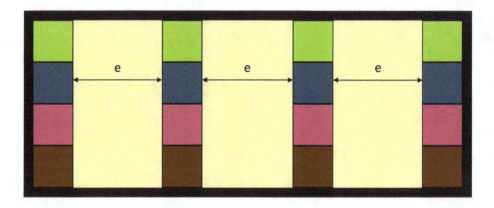

Try it yourself

CSS

```css
section {
  display: grid;
  justify-content: space-between;
  grid-template-columns: repeat(4, 40px);
  background-color: orange;
  margin: 10px;
}

div {
  border: 1px solid black;
  background-color: purple;
  color: white;
  padding: 10px;
  border-radius: 5px;
  text-align: center;
}
```

HTML

```html
<section>
  <div>1</div>
  <div>2</div>
  <div>3</div>
  <div>4</div>
  <div>5</div>
  <div>6</div>
  <div>7</div>
  <div>8</div>
</section>
```

Live Example[14]

justify-content: space-around

`space-around` assigns equal spacing to each side of a grid container's columns.

Therefore, the space before the first column and after the last one is half the width of the space between each pair of columns.

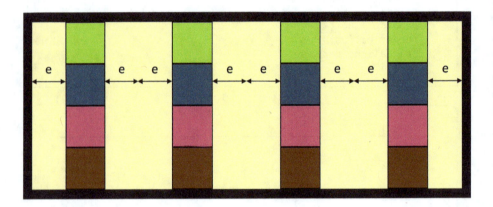

Try it yourself

CSS

```css
section {
  display: grid;
  justify-content: space-around;
  grid-template-columns: repeat(4, 40px);
  background-color: orange;
  margin: 10px;
}

div {
  border: 1px solid black;
  background-color: purple;
  color: white;
  padding: 10px;
  border-radius: 5px;
  text-align: center;
}
```

HTML

```html
<section>
  <div>1</div>
  <div>2</div>
  <div>3</div>
  <div>4</div>
  <div>5</div>
  <div>6</div>
  <div>7</div>
  <div>8</div>
</section>
```

Live Example[15]

justify-content: space-evenly

space-evenly assigns even spacing to both ends of a grid container and between its columns.

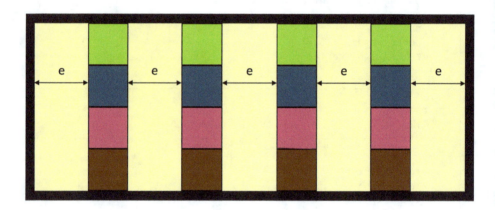

Try it yourself

CSS

```css
section {
  display: grid;
  justify-content: space-evenly;
  grid-template-columns: repeat(4, 40px);
  background-color: orange;
  margin: 10px;
}

div {
  border: 1px solid black;
  background-color: purple;
  color: white;
  padding: 10px;
  border-radius: 5px;
  text-align: center;
}
```

HTML

```html
<section>
  <div>1</div>
  <div>2</div>
  <div>3</div>
  <div>4</div>
  <div>5</div>
  <div>6</div>
  <div>7</div>
  <div>8</div>
</section>
```

Live Example[16]

"Every artist was first an amateur."

– Ralph Waldo Emerson

justify-items Property

justify-items specify the default justify-self value for all the grid items.

justify-items property's values

1. stretch

2. start

3. center

4. end

justify-items: stretch

stretch is justify-items' default value. It stretches the grid container's items to fill their individual cells' row (inline) axis.

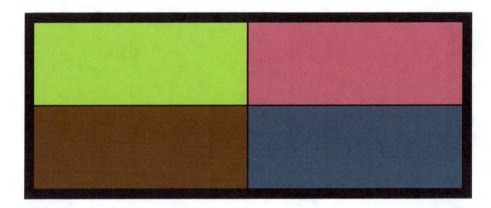

Try it yourself

CSS

```css
section {
  display: grid;
  justify-items: stretch;
  grid-template-columns: 1fr 1fr;
  background-color: orange;
  margin: 10px;
}

div {
  border: 1px solid black;
  background-color: purple;
  color: white;
  padding: 10px;
  border-radius: 5px;
}
```

HTML

```html
<section>
  <div>1</div>
  <div>2</div>
  <div>3</div>
  <div>4</div>
</section>
```

Live Example[17]

justify-items: start

start positions a grid container's items with the row-start edge of their individual cells' row axis.

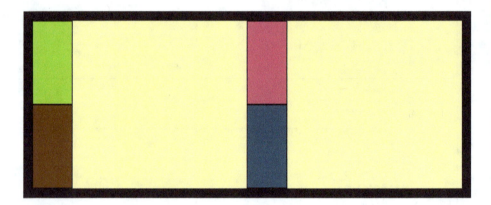

Try it yourself

CSS

```css
section {
  display: grid;
  justify-items: start;
  grid-template-columns: 1fr 1fr;
  background-color: orange;
  margin: 10px;
}

div {
  border: 1px solid black;
  background-color: purple;
  color: white;
  padding: 10px;
  border-radius: 5px;
}
```

HTML

```html
<section>
  <div>1</div>
  <div>2</div>
  <div>3</div>
  <div>4</div>
</section>
```

Live Example[18]

justify-items: center

center positions a grid container's items to the center of their individual cells' row axis.

Try it yourself

CSS

```css
section {
  display: grid;
  justify-items: center;
  grid-template-columns: 1fr 1fr;
  background-color: orange;
  margin: 10px;
}

div {
  border: 1px solid black;
  background-color: purple;
  color: white;
  padding: 10px;
  border-radius: 5px;
}
```

HTML

```html
<section>
  <div>1</div>
  <div>2</div>
  <div>3</div>
  <div>4</div>
</section>
```

Live Example[19]

justify-items: end

end positions a grid container's items with the row-end edge of their individual cells' row axis.

Try it yourself

CSS

```css
section {
  display: grid;
  justify-items: end;
  grid-template-columns: 1fr 1fr;
  background-color: orange;
  margin: 10px;
}

div {
  border: 1px solid black;
  background-color: purple;
  color: white;
  padding: 10px;
  border-radius: 5px;
}
```

HTML

```html
<section>
  <div>1</div>
  <div>2</div>
  <div>3</div>
  <div>4</div>
</section>
```

Live Example[20]

"Mount Everest, you beat me the first time, but I'll beat you the next time because you've grown all you are going to grow...and I'm still growing!"

– Edmund Hillary

align-content Property

`align-content` specifies how browsers should align a grid container's rows along the container's column axis.

The `align-content` property works only if the total row heights are less than the grid container's height. In other words, you need free space along the container's column axis to align its rows up or down.

Note: A column axis is sometimes called a *block axis*.

align-content property's values

1. stretch

2. start

3. center

4. end

5. space-between

6. space-around

7. space-evenly

align-content: stretch

stretch is align-content's default value. It stretches the grid container's rows to fill the grid's cross-axis.

Try it yourself

CSS

```css
section {
  display: grid;
  align-content: stretch;
  grid-template-columns: 1fr 1fr;
  background-color: orange;
  margin: 10px;
  height: 300px;
}

div {
  border: 1px solid black;
  background-color: purple;
  color: white;
  padding: 10px;
  border-radius: 5px;
}
```

HTML

```html
<section>
  <div>1</div>
  <div>2</div>
  <div>3</div>
  <div>4</div>
</section>
```

Live Example[21]

align-content: start

start aligns a grid container's rows with the column-start edge of the grid's column axis.

Try it yourself

CSS

```css
section {
  display: grid;
  align-content: start;
  grid-template-columns: 1fr 1fr;
  background-color: orange;
  margin: 10px;
  height: 300px;
}

div {
  border: 1px solid black;
  background-color: purple;
  color: white;
  padding: 10px;
  border-radius: 5px;
}
```

HTML

```html
<section>
  <div>1</div>
  <div>2</div>
  <div>3</div>
  <div>4</div>
</section>
```

Live Example[22]

align-content: center

center aligns a grid container's rows to the center of the grid's column axis.

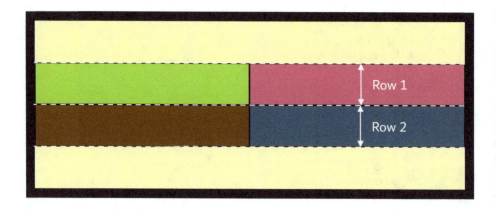

Try it yourself

CSS

```css
section {
  display: grid;
  align-content: center;
  grid-template-columns: 1fr 1fr;
  background-color: orange;
  margin: 10px;
  height: 300px;
}

div {
  border: 1px solid black;
  background-color: purple;
  color: white;
  padding: 10px;
  border-radius: 5px;
}
```

HTML

```html
<section>
  <div>1</div>
  <div>2</div>
  <div>3</div>
  <div>4</div>
</section>
```

Live Example[23]

align-content: end

end aligns a grid container's rows with the column-end edge of the grid's column axis.

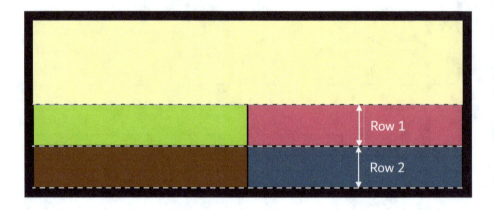

Try it yourself

CSS

```css
section {
  display: grid;
  align-content: end;
  grid-template-columns: 1fr 1fr;
  background-color: orange;
  margin: 10px;
  height: 300px;
}

div {
  border: 1px solid black;
  background-color: purple;
  color: white;
  padding: 10px;
  border-radius: 5px;
}
```

HTML

```html
<section>
  <div>1</div>
  <div>2</div>
  <div>3</div>
  <div>4</div>
</section>
```

Live Example[24]

align-content: space-between

`space-between` does the following:

- It aligns a grid container's first row with its column-start edge.

- It aligns the container's last row with the column-end edge.

- It creates even spacing between each pair of rows between the first and last row.

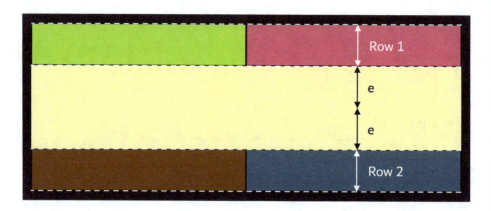

Try it yourself

CSS

```
section {
  display: grid;
  align-content: space-between;
  grid-template-columns: 1fr 1fr;
  background-color: orange;
  margin: 10px;
  height: 300px;
}

div {
  border: 1px solid black;
  background-color: purple;
  color: white;
  padding: 10px;
  border-radius: 5px;
}
```

HTML

```
<section>
  <div>1</div>
  <div>2</div>
  <div>3</div>
  <div>4</div>
</section>
```

Live Example[25]

align-content: space-around

space-around assigns equal spacing to each side of a grid container's rows.

Therefore, the space before the first row and after the last one is half the width of the space between each pair of rows.

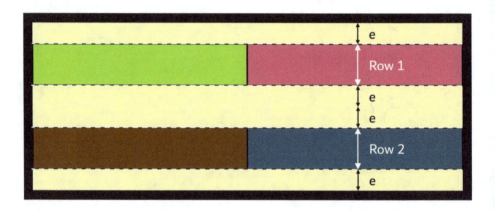

Try it yourself

CSS

```css
section {
  display: grid;
  align-content: space-around;
  grid-template-columns: 1fr 1fr;
  background-color: orange;
  margin: 10px;
  height: 300px;
}

div {
  border: 1px solid black;
  background-color: purple;
  color: white;
  padding: 10px;
  border-radius: 5px;
}
```

HTML

```html
<section>
  <div>1</div>
  <div>2</div>
  <div>3</div>
  <div>4</div>
</section>
```

Live Example[26]

align-content: space-evenly

space-evenly assigns even spacing to both ends of a grid container and between its rows.

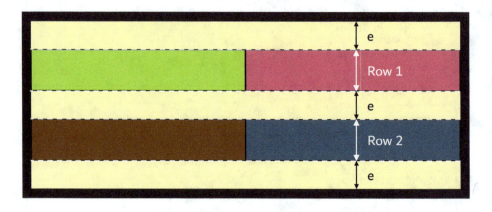

Try it yourself

CSS

```css
section {
  display: grid;
  align-content: space-evenly;
  grid-template-columns: 1fr 1fr;
  background-color: orange;
  margin: 10px;
  height: 300px;
}

div {
  border: 1px solid black;
  background-color: purple;
  color: white;
  padding: 10px;
  border-radius: 5px;
}
```

HTML

```html
<section>
  <div>1</div>
  <div>2</div>
  <div>3</div>
  <div>4</div>
</section>
```

Live Example[27]

"Victory is won not in miles but in inches. Win a little now, hold your ground, and later win a lot more."

– Louis L' Amour

align-items Property

`align-items` specify the default `align-self` value for all the grid items.

align-items property's values

1. stretch

2. start

3. center

4. end

align-items: stretch

stretch stretches the grid container's items to fill their individual cells' column (block) axis.

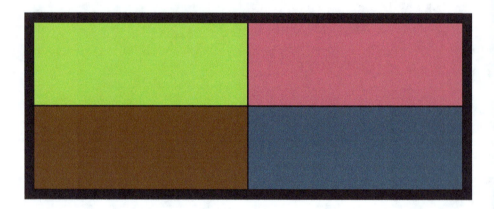

Try it yourself

CSS

```css
section {
  display: grid;
  align-items: stretch;
  grid-template-columns: 1fr 1fr;
  background-color: orange;
  margin: 10px;
  height: 400px;
}

div {
  border: 1px solid black;
  background-color: purple;
  color: white;
  padding: 10px;
  border-radius: 5px;
}
```

HTML

```html
<section>
  <div>1</div>
  <div>2</div>
  <div>3</div>
  <div>4</div>
</section>
```

Live Example[28]

align-items: start

start aligns a grid container's items with the column-start edge of their individual cells' column axis.

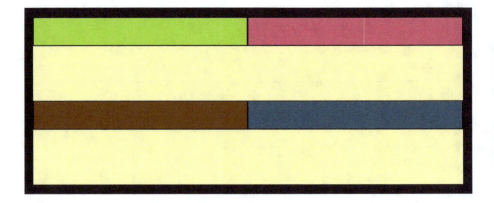

Try it yourself

CSS

```css
section {
  display: grid;
  align-items: start;
  grid-template-columns: 1fr 1fr;
  background-color: orange;
  margin: 10px;
  height: 400px;
}

div {
  border: 1px solid black;
  background-color: purple;
  color: white;
  padding: 10px;
  border-radius: 5px;
}
```

HTML

```html
<section>
  <div>1</div>
  <div>2</div>
  <div>3</div>
  <div>4</div>
</section>
```

Live Example[29]

align-items: center

`center` aligns a grid container's items to the center of their individual cells' column axis.

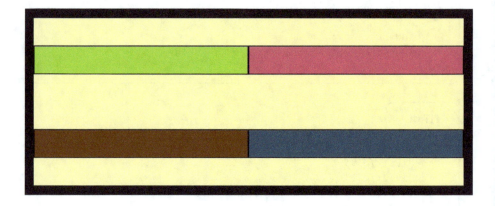

Try it yourself

CSS

```css
section {
  display: grid;
  align-items: center;
  grid-template-columns: 1fr 1fr;
  background-color: orange;
  margin: 10px;
  height: 400px;
}

div {
  border: 1px solid black;
  background-color: purple;
  color: white;
  padding: 10px;
  border-radius: 5px;
}
```

HTML

```html
<section>
  <div>1</div>
  <div>2</div>
  <div>3</div>
  <div>4</div>
</section>
```

Live Example[30]

align-items: end

end aligns a grid container's items with the column-end edge of their individual cells' column axis.

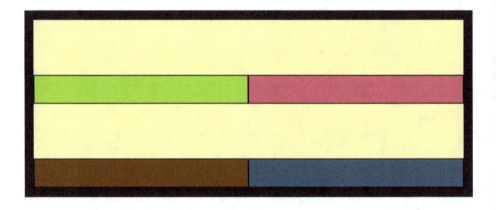

Try it yourself

CSS

```css
section {
  display: grid;
  align-items: end;
  grid-template-columns: 1fr 1fr;
  background-color: orange;
  margin: 10px;
  height: 400px;
}

div {
  border: 1px solid black;
  background-color: purple;
  color: white;
  padding: 10px;
  border-radius: 5px;
}
```

HTML

```html
<section>
  <div>1</div>
  <div>2</div>
  <div>3</div>
  <div>4</div>
</section>
```

Live Example[31]

Grid Item's Properties

A grid item's properties specify how browsers should layout a specified item within the grid box model.

We define a grid item's property on the item, not its container.

Types of grid items properties

1. justify-self

2. align-self

3. grid-column-start

4. grid-column-end

5. grid-column

6. grid-row-start

7. grid-row-end

8. grid-row

9. grid-area

10. grid-template-areas

justify-self Property

`justify-self` specifies how browsers should position the selected grid item along its cell's row (inline) axis.

`justify-self` affects only the selected grid item—not all the grid's items. It also overrides the `justify-items` property.

justify-self property's values

1. stretch

2. start

3. center

4. end

justify-self: stretch

stretch stretches the selected grid item to fill its cell's row (inline) axis.

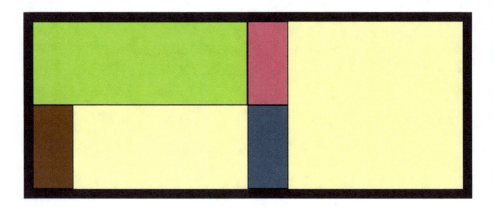

Try it yourself

CSS

```css
section {
  display: grid;
  justify-items: start;
  grid-template-columns: 1fr 1fr;
  background-color: orange;
  margin: 10px;
}

div {
  border: 1px solid black;
  background-color: purple;
  color: white;
  padding: 10px;
  border-radius: 5px;
}

.grid-item1 {
  justify-self: stretch;
}
```

HTML

```html
<section>
  <div class="grid-item1">1</div>
  <div class="grid-item2">2</div>
  <div class="grid-item3">3</div>
  <div class="grid-item4">4</div>
</section>
```

Live Example[32]

justify-self: start

start positions the selected grid item with the row-start edge of its cell's row axis.

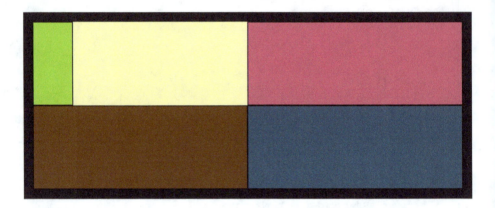

Try it yourself

CSS

```css
section {
  display: grid;
  grid-template-columns: 1fr 1fr;
  background-color: orange;
  margin: 10px;
}

div {
  border: 1px solid black;
  background-color: purple;
  color: white;
  padding: 10px;
  border-radius: 5px;
}

.grid-item1 {
  justify-self: start;
}
```

HTML

```html
<section>
  <div class="grid-item1">1</div>
  <div class="grid-item2">2</div>
  <div class="grid-item3">3</div>
  <div class="grid-item4">4</div>
</section>
```

Live Example[33]

justify-self: center

center positions the selected grid item to the center of its cell's row axis.

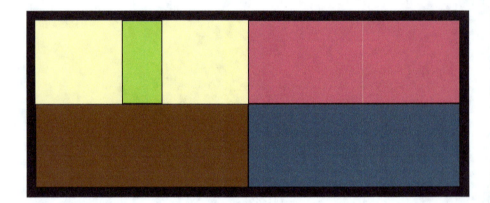

Try it yourself

CSS

```css
section {
  display: grid;
  grid-template-columns: 1fr 1fr;
  background-color: orange;
  margin: 10px;
}

div {
  border: 1px solid black;
  background-color: purple;
  color: white;
  padding: 10px;
  border-radius: 5px;
}

.grid-item1 {
  justify-self: center;
}
```

HTML

```html
<section>
  <div class="grid-item1">1</div>
  <div class="grid-item2">2</div>
  <div class="grid-item3">3</div>
  <div class="grid-item4">4</div>
</section>
```

Live Example[34]

justify-self: end

end positions the selected grid item with the row-end edge of its cell's row axis.

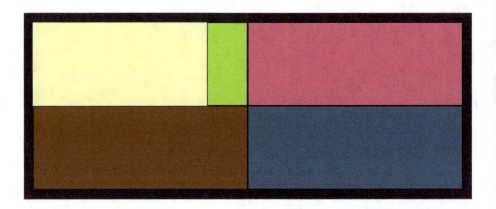

Try it yourself

CSS

```css
section {
  display: grid;
  grid-template-columns: 1fr 1fr;
  background-color: orange;
  margin: 10px;
}

div {
  border: 1px solid black;
  background-color: purple;
  color: white;
  padding: 10px;
  border-radius: 5px;
}

.grid-item1 {
  justify-self: end;
}
```

HTML

```html
<section>
  <div class="grid-item1">1</div>
  <div class="grid-item2">2</div>
  <div class="grid-item3">3</div>
  <div class="grid-item4">4</div>
</section>
```

Live Example[35]

"Great things are done by a series of small things brought together."

— Vincent Van Gogh

align-self Property

align-self specifies how browsers should align the selected grid item along its cell's column (block) axis.

align-self affects only the selected grid item—not all the grid's items. It also overrides the align-items property.

align-self property's values

1. stretch

2. start

3. center

4. end

align-self: stretch

stretch stretches the selected grid item to fill its cell's column (block) axis.

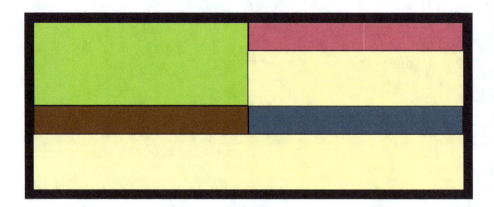

Try it yourself

```css
section {
  display: grid;
  align-items: start;
  grid-template-columns: 1fr 1fr;
  background-color: orange;
  margin: 10px;
  height: 400px;
}

div {
  border: 1px solid black;
  background-color: purple;
  color: white;
  padding: 10px;
  border-radius: 5px;
}

.grid-item1 {
  align-self: stretch;
}
```

CSS

HTML

```html
<section>
  <div class="grid-item1">1</div>
  <div class="grid-item2">2</div>
  <div class="grid-item3">3</div>
  <div class="grid-item4">4</div>
</section>
```

Live Example[36]

align-self: start

start aligns the selected grid item with the column-start edge of its cell's column axis.

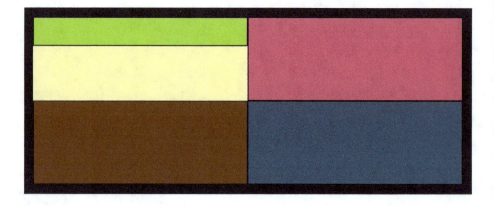

Try it yourself

CSS

```css
section {
  display: grid;
  grid-template-columns: 1fr 1fr;
  background-color: orange;
  margin: 10px;
  height: 400px;
}

div {
  border: 1px solid black;
  background-color: purple;
  color: white;
  padding: 10px;
  border-radius: 5px;
}

.grid-item1 {
  align-self: start;
}
```

HTML

```html
<section>
  <div class="grid-item1">1</div>
  <div class="grid-item2">2</div>
  <div class="grid-item3">3</div>
  <div class="grid-item4">4</div>
</section>
```

Live Example[37]

align-self: center

center aligns the selected grid item to the center of its cell's column axis.

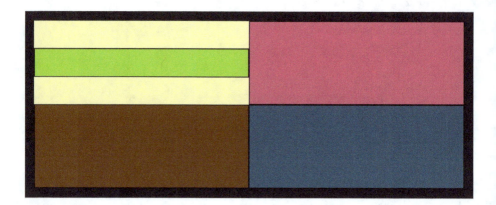

Try it yourself

CSS

```css
section {
  display: grid;
  grid-template-columns: 1fr 1fr;
  background-color: orange;
  margin: 10px;
  height: 400px;
}

div {
  border: 1px solid black;
  background-color: purple;
  color: white;
  padding: 10px;
  border-radius: 5px;
}

.grid-item1 {
  align-self: center;
}
```

HTML

```html
<section>
  <div class="grid-item1">1</div>
  <div class="grid-item2">2</div>
  <div class="grid-item3">3</div>
  <div class="grid-item4">4</div>
</section>
```

Live Example[38]

align-self: end

end aligns the selected grid item with the column-end edge of its cell's column axis.

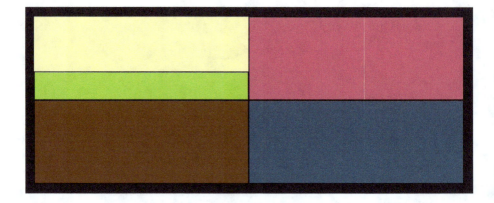

Try it yourself

CSS

```css
section {
  display: grid;
  grid-template-columns: 1fr 1fr;
  background-color: orange;
  margin: 10px;
  height: 400px;
}

div {
  border: 1px solid black;
  background-color: purple;
  color: white;
  padding: 10px;
  border-radius: 5px;
}

.grid-item1 {
  align-self: end;
}
```

HTML

```html
<section>
  <div class="grid-item1">1</div>
  <div class="grid-item2">2</div>
  <div class="grid-item3">3</div>
  <div class="grid-item4">4</div>
</section>
```

Live Example[39]

"In trying times, don't stop trying."

– John Mason

CSS Grid Lines

CSS grid lines are the lines browsers create on a grid container when you define the `grid-template-columns` or `grid-template-rows` property.

Note: We call the space between any two grid lines a *grid track*.

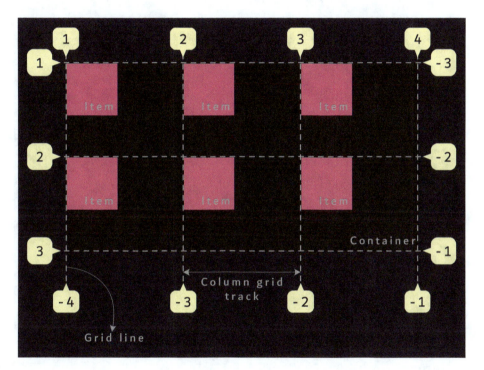

Types of CSS grid lines

1. Grid column lines
2. Grid row lines

Grid Column Line

Grid column lines are the lines browsers create on a grid container's column (block) axis when you define the `grid-template-columns` property.

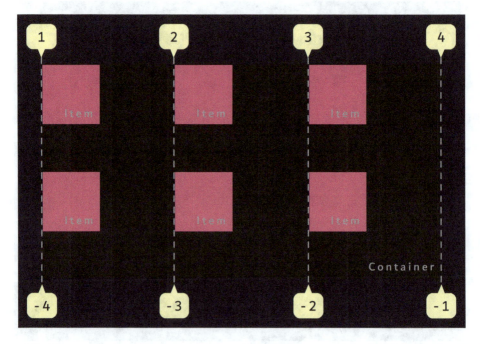

Note:

- The numbering of the grid column lines starts from number one (1) at the grid container's column-start edge.

- Suppose your writing language script is horizontal left-to-right—like English. In that case, your grid column line 1 will be at the top-left of the grid container.

- Browsers use negative numbers to indicate end lines. For instance, the last column line will get a -1 tag, while the third from the last line gets a -3 label.

Grid Row Line

Grid row lines are the lines browsers create on a grid container's row (inline) axis when you define the `grid-template-rows` property.

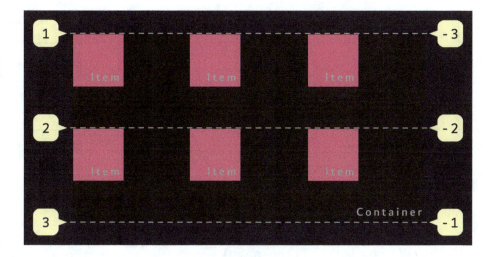

Note:

- The numbering of the grid row lines starts from number one (1) at the grid container's row-start edge.

- Browsers use negative numbers to indicate end lines. For instance, the last row line will get a -1 tag, while the third from the last line gets a -3 label.

- Follow Firefox's <u>CSS Grid Inspector guide</u>[40] to learn how to examine grid lines on your browser's DevTool.

How to Name Grid Lines

You can name some (or all) of your grid lines by specifying the
name inside square brackets ([ ]) while defining the number and
widths of your grid container's columns or rows.

Syntax

```css
element {
  grid-template-columns:
    [first-line] 20px [second-line] 50px [last-line];
}
```

In the CSS snippet above,

- We defined a two-columns grid container with widths of
  20px and 50px respectively.

- We used the [line-name] syntax to name the grid
  container's lines.

Try it yourself

CSS

```css
section {
  display: grid;
  grid-template-columns: 1fr 1fr [third-line] 1fr;
  background-color: orange;
  margin: 50px;
  min-height: 300px;
}

div {
  border: 1px solid black;
  background-color: purple;
  color: white;
  padding: 20px;
  border-radius: 5px;
}

.grid-item1 {
  grid-column-start: third-line;
}
```

HTML

```html
<section>
  <div class="grid-item1">1</div>
  <div class="grid-item2">2</div>
  <div class="grid-item3">3</div>
  <div class="grid-item4">4</div>
  <div class="grid-item5">5</div>
  <div class="grid-item6">6</div>
  <div class="grid-item7">7</div>
  <div class="grid-item8">8</div>
  <div class="grid-item9">9</div>
</section>
```

Live Example[41]

"The most common trait I have found in all people that are successful is that they have conquered the temptation to give up."

– Peter Lowe

grid-column-start Property

`grid-column-start` specifies where the selected grid item should start (or span) along the grid container's row (inline) axis.

grid-column-start property's values

1. auto

2. <line-number>

3. span <number>

grid-column-start: auto

auto auto-starts the selected grid item following the normal column flow.

Try it yourself

CSS

```css
section {
  display: grid;
  grid-template-columns: 1fr 1fr 1fr;
  background-color: orange;
  margin: 50px;
  min-height: 300px;
}

div {
  border: 1px solid black;
  background-color: purple;
  color: white;
  padding: 20px;
  border-radius: 5px;
}

.grid-item1 {
  grid-column-start: auto;
}
```

HTML

```html
<section>
  <div class="grid-item1">1</div>
  <div class="grid-item2">2</div>
  <div class="grid-item3">3</div>
  <div class="grid-item4">4</div>
  <div class="grid-item5">5</div>
  <div class="grid-item6">6</div>
  <div class="grid-item7">7</div>
  <div class="grid-item8">8</div>
  <div class="grid-item9">9</div>
</section>
```

Live Example[42]

grid-column-start: line-number

`line-number` starts the selected grid item at the specified column line.

Try it yourself

```css
section {
  display: grid;
  grid-template-columns: 1fr 1fr 1fr;
  background-color: orange;
  margin: 50px;
  min-height: 300px;
}

div {
  border: 1px solid black;
  background-color: purple;
  color: white;
  padding: 20px;
  border-radius: 5px;
}

.grid-item1 {
  grid-column-start: 3;
}
```

HTML

```html
<section>
  <div class="grid-item1">1</div>
  <div class="grid-item2">2</div>
  <div class="grid-item3">3</div>
  <div class="grid-item4">4</div>
  <div class="grid-item5">5</div>
  <div class="grid-item6">6</div>
  <div class="grid-item7">7</div>
  <div class="grid-item8">8</div>
  <div class="grid-item9">9</div>
</section>
```

Live Example[43]

grid-column-start: span number

span number spans the selected grid item across the specified number of columns.

Try it yourself

CSS

```css
section {
  display: grid;
  grid-template-columns: 1fr 1fr 1fr;
  background-color: orange;
  margin: 50px;
  min-height: 300px;
}

div {
  border: 1px solid black;
  background-color: purple;
  color: white;
  padding: 20px;
  border-radius: 5px;
}

.grid-item1 {
  grid-column-start: span 2;
}
```

HTML

```html
<section>
  <div class="grid-item1">1</div>
  <div class="grid-item2">2</div>
  <div class="grid-item3">3</div>
  <div class="grid-item4">4</div>
  <div class="grid-item5">5</div>
  <div class="grid-item6">6</div>
  <div class="grid-item7">7</div>
  <div class="grid-item8">8</div>
  <div class="grid-item9">9</div>
</section>
```

Live Example[44]

grid-column-end Property

`grid-column-end` specifies where the selected grid item should end (or span) along the grid container's row (inline) axis.

grid-column-end property's values

1. auto

2. <line-number>

3. span <number>

grid-column-end: auto

auto auto-ends the selected grid item following the normal column flow.

Try it yourself

CSS

```css
section {
  display: grid;
  grid-template-columns: 1fr 1fr 1fr;
  background-color: orange;
  margin: 50px;
  min-height: 300px;
}

div {
  border: 1px solid black;
  background-color: purple;
  color: white;
  padding: 20px;
  border-radius: 5px;
}

.grid-item1 {
  grid-column-end: auto;
}
```

HTML

```html
<section>
  <div class="grid-item1">1</div>
  <div class="grid-item2">2</div>
  <div class="grid-item3">3</div>
  <div class="grid-item4">4</div>
  <div class="grid-item5">5</div>
  <div class="grid-item6">6</div>
  <div class="grid-item7">7</div>
  <div class="grid-item8">8</div>
  <div class="grid-item9">9</div>
</section>
```

Live Example[45]

grid-column-end: line-number

`line-number` ends the selected grid item at the specified column line.

Try it yourself

CSS

```css
section {
    display: grid;
    grid-template-columns: 1fr 1fr 1fr;
    background-color: orange;
    margin: 50px;
    min-height: 300px;
}

div {
    border: 1px solid black;
    background-color: purple;
    color: white;
    padding: 20px;
    border-radius: 5px;
}

.grid-item1 {
    grid-column-start: 1;
    grid-column-end: 3;
}
```

HTML

```html
<section>
    <div class="grid-item1">1</div>
    <div class="grid-item2">2</div>
    <div class="grid-item3">3</div>
    <div class="grid-item4">4</div>
    <div class="grid-item5">5</div>
    <div class="grid-item6">6</div>
    <div class="grid-item7">7</div>
    <div class="grid-item8">8</div>
    <div class="grid-item9">9</div>
</section>
```

Live Example[46]

grid-column-end: span number

span number spans the selected grid item across the specified number of columns.

Try it yourself

CSS

```css
section {
  display: grid;
  grid-template-columns: 1fr 1fr 1fr;
  background-color: orange;
  margin: 50px;
  min-height: 300px;
}

div {
  border: 1px solid black;
  background-color: purple;
  color: white;
  padding: 20px;
  border-radius: 5px;
}

.grid-item1 {
  grid-column-start: 2;
  grid-column-end: span 2;
}
```

HTML

```html
<section>
  <div class="grid-item1">1</div>
  <div class="grid-item2">2</div>
  <div class="grid-item3">3</div>
  <div class="grid-item4">4</div>
  <div class="grid-item5">5</div>
  <div class="grid-item6">6</div>
  <div class="grid-item7">7</div>
  <div class="grid-item8">8</div>
  <div class="grid-item9">9</div>
</section>
```

Live Example[47]

grid-row-start Property

grid-row-start specifies where the selected grid item should start (or span) along the grid container's column (block) axis.

grid-row-start property's values

1. auto

2. <line-number>

3. span <number>

grid-row-start: auto

auto auto-starts the selected grid item following the normal row flow.

Try it yourself

CSS

```css
section {
  display: grid;
  grid-template-columns: 1fr 1fr 1fr;
  grid-template-rows: 1fr 1fr 1fr;
  background-color: orange;
  margin: 50px;
  min-height: 300px;
}

div {
  border: 1px solid black;
  background-color: purple;
  color: white;
  padding: 20px;
  border-radius: 5px;
}

.grid-item1 {
  grid-row-start: auto;
}
```

HTML

```html
<section>
  <div class="grid-item1">1</div>
  <div class="grid-item2">2</div>
  <div class="grid-item3">3</div>
  <div class="grid-item4">4</div>
  <div class="grid-item5">5</div>
  <div class="grid-item6">6</div>
  <div class="grid-item7">7</div>
  <div class="grid-item8">8</div>
  <div class="grid-item9">9</div>
</section>
```

Live Example[48]

grid-row-start: line-number

`line-number` starts the selected grid item at the specified row line.

Try it yourself

CSS

```css
section {
  display: grid;
  grid-template-columns: 1fr 1fr 1fr;
  grid-template-rows: 1fr 1fr 1fr;
  background-color: orange;
  margin: 50px;
  min-height: 300px;
}

div {
  border: 1px solid black;
  background-color: purple;
  color: white;
  padding: 20px;
  border-radius: 5px;
}

.grid-item1 {
  grid-row-start: 3;
}
```

HTML

```html
<section>
  <div class="grid-item1">1</div>
  <div class="grid-item2">2</div>
  <div class="grid-item3">3</div>
  <div class="grid-item4">4</div>
  <div class="grid-item5">5</div>
  <div class="grid-item6">6</div>
  <div class="grid-item7">7</div>
  <div class="grid-item8">8</div>
  <div class="grid-item9">9</div>
</section>
```

Live Example[49]

grid-row-start: span number

span number spans the selected grid item across the specified number of rows.

Try it yourself

CSS

```css
section {
  display: grid;
  grid-template-columns: 1fr 1fr 1fr;
  grid-template-rows: 1fr 1fr 1fr 1fr;
  background-color: orange;
  margin: 50px;
  min-height: 300px;
}

div {
  border: 1px solid black;
  background-color: purple;
  color: white;
  padding: 20px;
  border-radius: 5px;
}

.grid-item1 {
  grid-row-start: span 2;
}
```

HTML

```html
<section>
  <div class="grid-item1">1</div>
  <div class="grid-item2">2</div>
  <div class="grid-item3">3</div>
  <div class="grid-item4">4</div>
  <div class="grid-item5">5</div>
  <div class="grid-item6">6</div>
  <div class="grid-item7">7</div>
  <div class="grid-item8">8</div>
  <div class="grid-item9">9</div>
</section>
```

Live Example[50]

grid-row-end Property

grid-row-end specifies where the selected grid item should end (or span) along the grid container's column (block) axis.

grid-row-end property's values

1. auto

2. <line-number>

3. span <number>

grid-row-end: auto

auto auto-ends the selected grid item following the normal row flow.

Try it yourself

CSS

```css
section {
  display: grid;
  grid-template-columns: 1fr 1fr 1fr;
  grid-template-rows: 1fr 1fr 1fr 1fr;
  background-color: orange;
  margin: 50px;
  min-height: 300px;
}

div {
  border: 1px solid black;
  background-color: purple;
  color: white;
  padding: 20px;
  border-radius: 5px;
}

.grid-item1 {
  grid-row-end: auto;
}
```

HTML

```html
<section>
  <div class="grid-item1">1</div>
  <div class="grid-item2">2</div>
  <div class="grid-item3">3</div>
  <div class="grid-item4">4</div>
  <div class="grid-item5">5</div>
  <div class="grid-item6">6</div>
  <div class="grid-item7">7</div>
  <div class="grid-item8">8</div>
  <div class="grid-item9">9</div>
</section>
```

Live Example[51]

grid-row-end: line-number

`line-number` ends the selected grid item at the specified row line.

Try it yourself

CSS

```css
section {
  display: grid;
  grid-template-columns: 1fr 1fr 1fr;
  grid-template-rows: 1fr 1fr 1fr;
  background-color: orange;
  margin: 50px;
  min-height: 300px;
}

div {
  border: 1px solid black;
  background-color: purple;
  color: white;
  padding: 20px;
  border-radius: 5px;
}

.grid-item1 {
  grid-row-start: 1;
  grid-row-end: 5;
}
```

HTML

```html
<section>
  <div class="grid-item1">1</div>
  <div class="grid-item2">2</div>
  <div class="grid-item3">3</div>
  <div class="grid-item4">4</div>
  <div class="grid-item5">5</div>
  <div class="grid-item6">6</div>
  <div class="grid-item7">7</div>
  <div class="grid-item8">8</div>
  <div class="grid-item9">9</div>
</section>
```

Live Example[52]

grid-row-end: span number

span number spans the selected grid item across the specified number of rows.

Try it yourself

CSS

```css
section {
  display: grid;
  grid-template-columns: 1fr 1fr 1fr;
  grid-template-rows: 1fr 1fr 1fr 1fr;
  background-color: orange;
  margin: 50px;
  min-height: 300px;
}

div {
  border: 1px solid black;
  background-color: purple;
  color: white;
  padding: 20px;
  border-radius: 5px;
}

.grid-item1 {
  grid-row-end: span 3;
}
```

HTML

```html
<section>
  <div class="grid-item1">1</div>
  <div class="grid-item2">2</div>
  <div class="grid-item3">3</div>
  <div class="grid-item4">4</div>
  <div class="grid-item5">5</div>
  <div class="grid-item6">6</div>
  <div class="grid-item7">7</div>
  <div class="grid-item8">8</div>
  <div class="grid-item9">9</div>
</section>
```

Live Example[53]

Additional Resources

Below are helpful links to other supplementary content on the grid layout module.

- grid-column[54]

- grid-row[55]

- grid-area[56]

- grid-template-areas[57]

- column-gap[58]

- row-gap[59]

- gap[60]

- minmax()[61]

- repeat()[62]

GET YOUR FREEBIE

If you didn't download it earlier, I would like you to have my Git Cheat Sheet **100% FREE!**

DOWNLOAD IT HERE:

https://www.subscribepage.com/git-cheatsheet

Endnotes

¹ Box model (https://codesweetly.com/css-box-model)

² Flexbox (https://codesweetly.com/css-flexbox-explained)

³ HTML element (https://codesweetly.com/web-tech-terms-h#html-element)

⁴ CSS display property (https://codesweetly.com/css-display-property)

⁵ Block-level HTML elements (https://developer.mozilla.org/en-US/docs/Web/HTML/Block-level_elements)

⁶ Inline-level HTML elements (https://developer.mozilla.org/en-US/docs/Web/HTML/Inline_elements)

⁷ display: grid live example (https://stackblitz.com/edit/js-5ggr6k?file=style.css)

⁸ display: inline-grid live example (https://stackblitz.com/edit/js-ekpbac?file=style.css)

⁹ grid-template-columns live example (https://stackblitz.com/edit/js-xaop69?file=style.css)

¹⁰ grid-template-rows live example (https://stackblitz.com/edit/js-e5vtot?file=style.css)

¹¹ justify-content: start live example (https://stackblitz.com/edit/js-rkwg9r?file=style.css)

¹² justify-content: center live example (https://stackblitz.com/edit/js-ft8n3n?file=style.css)

¹³ justify-content: end live example (https://stackblitz.com/edit/js-zzaxjf?file=style.css)

¹⁴ justify-content: space-between live example (https://stackblitz.com/edit/js-ajbrex?file=style.css)

¹⁵ justify-content: space-around live example (https://stackblitz.com/edit/js-qnla5x?file=style.css)

Endnotes

[16] justify-content: space-evenly live example (https://stackblitz.com/edit/js-vnd1u3?file=style.css)

[17] justify-content: stretch live example (https://stackblitz.com/edit/js-dedmgi?file=style.css)

[18] justify-content: start live example (https://stackblitz.com/edit/js-zdzwmb?file=style.css)

[19] justify-content: center live example (https://stackblitz.com/edit/js-dsgyni?file=style.css)

[20] justify-content: end live example (https://stackblitz.com/edit/js-pcenzt?file=style.css)

[21] align-content: stretch live example (https://stackblitz.com/edit/js-qjtcla?file=style.css)

[22] align-content: start live example (https://stackblitz.com/edit/js-cbmgr1?file=style.css)

[23] align-content: center live example (https://stackblitz.com/edit/js-83kj8v?file=style.css)

[24] align-content: end live example (https://stackblitz.com/edit/js-lc1lus?file=style.css)

[25] align-content: space-between live example (https://stackblitz.com/edit/js-ieqvih?file=style.css)

[26] align-content: space-around live example (https://stackblitz.com/edit/js-eyzta5?file=style.css)

[27] align-content: space-evenly live example (https://stackblitz.com/edit/js-il5vu1?file=style.css)

[28] align-items: stretch live example (https://stackblitz.com/edit/js-fia3ra?file=style.css)

[29] align-items: start live example (https://stackblitz.com/edit/js-achetg?file=style.css)

[30] align-items: center live example (https://stackblitz.com/edit/js-cmqydk?file=style.css)

Endnotes

[31] align-items: end live example (https://stackblitz.com/edit/js-jei1qv?file=style.css)

[32] justify-self: stretch live example (https://stackblitz.com/edit/js-82a3ep?file=style.css)

[33] justify-self: start live example (https://stackblitz.com/edit/js-cnz92l?file=style.css)

[34] justify-self: center live example (https://stackblitz.com/edit/js-9kspmx?file=style.css)

[35] justify-self: end live example (https://stackblitz.com/edit/js-xschhb?file=style.css)

[36] align-self: stretch live example (https://stackblitz.com/edit/js-unnbb9?file=style.css)

[37] align-self: start live example (https://stackblitz.com/edit/js-ytttz4?file=style.css)

[38] align-self: center live example (https://stackblitz.com/edit/js-fpv4ed?file=style.css)

[39] align-self: end live example (https://stackblitz.com/edit/js-vvmwzv?file=style.css)

[40] CSS grid inspector guide (https://firefox-source-docs.mozilla.org/devtools-user/page_inspector/how_to/examine_grid_layouts/index.html)

[41] How to name grid lines live example (https://stackblitz.com/edit/js-3t7sth?file=style.css)

[42] grid-column-start: auto live example (https://stackblitz.com/edit/js-rvhhxh?file=style.css)

[43] grid-column-start: line-number live example (https://stackblitz.com/edit/js-ep6zgd?file=style.css)

[44] grid-column-start: span number live example (https://stackblitz.com/edit/js-w1nw8k?file=style.css)

[45] grid-column-end: auto live example (https://stackblitz.com/edit/js-1mmxhp?file=style.css)

[46] grid-column-end: line-number live example (https://stackblitz.com/edit/js-hjcfhc?file=style.css)

[47] grid-column-end: span number live example (https://stackblitz.com/edit/js-yhe3ew?file=style.css)

[48] grid-row-start: auto live example (https://stackblitz.com/edit/js-qthpn6?file=style.css)

[49] grid-row-start: line-number live example (https://stackblitz.com/edit/js-phrjcb?file=style.css)

[50] grid-row-start: span number live example (https://stackblitz.com/edit/js-5bchie?file=style.css)

[51] grid-row-end: auto live example (https://stackblitz.com/edit/js-w1rpy8?file=style.css)

[52] grid-row-end: line-number live example (https://stackblitz.com/edit/js-wps8a3?file=style.css)

[53] grid-row-end: span number live example (https://stackblitz.com/edit/js-skcbxf?file=style.css)

[54] grid-column CSS property (https://codesweetly.com/css-grid-column-property)

[55] grid-row CSS property (https://codesweetly.com/css-grid-row-property)

[56] grid-area CSS property (https://codesweetly.com/css-grid-area-property)

[57] grid-template-areas CSS property (https://codesweetly.com/css-grid-template-areas-property)

[58] column-gap CSS property (https://codesweetly.com/css-column-gap-property)

[59] row-gap CSS property (https://codesweetly.com/css-row-gap-property)

[60] gap CSS property (https://codesweetly.com/css-gap-property)

[61] minmax() CSS function (https://codesweetly.com/css-minmax-function)

[62] repeat() CSS function (https://codesweetly.com/css-repeat-function)

Other CodeSweetly Books...

CSS Flexbox: Complete Guide

Available at Amazon
(https://www.amazon.com/dp/
B0BN9DD7QF)

Visual Flexbox: Quick Guide

Available at Amazon
(https://www.amazon.com/dp/
B0BMZBNRD5)

React Explained Clearly

Available at Amazon
(https://www.amazon.com/dp/
B09KYGDQYW)

C<&>DESWEETLY

CodeSweetly exists specifically to help make coding so easy and fun to learn.

Visit codesweetly.com to learn web technology topics with simplified articles, images, and cheat sheets.